THE HISTORY OF THE OAKLAND RAIDERS

Published by Creative Education
123 South Broad Street
Mankato, Minnesota 56001
Creative Education is an imprint of The Creative Company.

DESIGN AND PRODUCTION BY **EVANSDAY DESIGN**

LIBRARY OF CONGRESS CATALOGING-IN-PUBLICATION DATA

Frisch, Aaron.
The history of the Oakland Raiders / by Aaron Frisch.
p. cm. — (NFL today)
Summary: Traces the history of the professional football team, describing its
three Super Bowl wins and the exploits of such legendary players as Jim Otto,
Ken "the Snake" Stabler, Jack "the Assassin" Tatum, and Bo Jackson.
ISBN 1-58341-308-1
1. Oakland Raiders (Football team)—History—Juvenile literature. [1. Oakland
Raiders (Football team)—History. 2. Football—History.] I. Title. II. Series.

GV956.O24F75 2003
796.332'64'0979494—dc22   2003062615

First edition

9 8 7 6 5 4 3 2 1

COVER PHOTO: wide receiver Jerry Porter

PHOTOGRAPHS BY
AP/Wide World Photos, Corbis (Bettmann, Brad Mangin/NewSport), Getty Images, SportsChrome USA

RAIDERS

Aaron Frisch

THE CITY OF **OAKLAND**, CALIFORNIA, SITS ALONG THE EAST SIDE OF THE SAN FRANCISCO BAY. FOUNDED IN 1854 DURING THE GREAT CALIFORNIA GOLD RUSH, OAKLAND GREW SLOWLY IN THE SHADOW OF ITS SISTER CITY SAN FRANCISCO, WHICH IS LOCATED JUST THREE MILES ACROSS THE BAY. TODAY OAKLAND IS ONE OF THE BUSIEST SHIPPING PORTS IN THE WORLD AND IS ALSO KNOWN AS THE HOMETOWN OF FAMOUS ADVENTURE WRITER JACK LONDON.

OAKLAND HAS LONG HAD A WINNING PROFESSIONAL SPORTS TRADITION THAT INCLUDES THE GOLDEN STATE WARRIORS BASKETBALL TEAM AND OAKLAND ATHLETICS BASEBALL TEAM. IN EARLY 1960, THE CITY WELCOMED YET ANOTHER PRO FRANCHISE: A FOOTBALL TEAM IN THE NEW AMERICAN FOOTBALL LEAGUE (AFL). SEEKING TO CREATE A FIERCE IMAGE, THE OWNERS OF THE NEW FRANCHISE DECKED OUT THEIR PLAYERS IN UNIFORMS OF BLACK AND SILVER AND NAMED THEM THE RAIDERS.

[Kicker George Blanda]

OAKLAND WAS THE last city to be awarded an AFL franchise, and its first few seasons were painful ones. In 1960, 1961, and 1962, the young Raiders—who featured such players as running back Clem Daniels and corner-back Fred Williamson—went a collective 9–33. Things were bleak, but at least the Raiders had one star around whom they could build: center Jim Otto.

AL DAVIS
AMERICAN
FOOTBALL
LEAGUE
COACH OF THE
YEAR
1963
PRESENTED BY
PRO FOOTBALL
ILLUSTRATED

Otto was a terrific player and a steady leader whom many football fans still remember by his strange jersey number: oo. Some National Football League (NFL) players and football experts wondered why such a talented player would sign on in the AFL, a league most considered to be inferior to the NFL. "I could make some NFL clubs, I know," Otto said. "But it's more of an honor and distinction to be an original member of a brand new league. That's why I chose to play with the Oakland Raiders."

Things improved in Oakland in 1963 when a young coach named Al Davis took over. Davis brought new ideas and a new level of energy to the franchise. And over the next four decades, Davis would become the face of the Raiders, rising to general manager and then owner of the team. Upon his arrival, Davis instructed his team to play with two "P"s: pride and poise. "Poise is the secret," he announced. "No matter what the scoreboard says, keep your poise."

With Davis leading them, the Raiders took off. They jumped to 10–4 in 1963 and then continued to add talent. By 1967, Oakland had a bunch of outstanding players, including quarterback Daryle Lamonica, guard Gene Upshaw, receiver Fred Biletnikoff, and cornerback Willie Brown. Behind these players, the 1967 Raiders went 13–1

Seemingly indestructible standout Jim Otto was the Raiders' starting center for 308 straight games.

Guard Gene Upshaw was a fearsome run blocker. ^

Fred Biletnikoff became famous for his sure hands ^

and beat the Houston Oilers for the AFL championship, a victory that put Oakland in the Super Bowl against the NFL champion Green Bay Packers. (In those days, the Super Bowl was a contest between the AFL and NFL champs, an arrangement Davis helped to set up.)

The young Raiders lost to Green Bay coach Vince Lombardi and his veteran Packers in the Super Bowl, but Oakland had established itself as a force. When the Raiders went 12–1–1 in 1969, the final season before the AFL merged with the NFL, it was obvious that the 1970s would be a special time in Oakland.

THE RAIDERS WERE led by coach John Madden for most of the 1970s. Madden, who would later become a popular television sportscaster, gave the Raiders a new attitude when he arrived in 1969. "I had a philosophy," the talkative coach explained. "I really liked my players. I liked them as people. I made a point to talk to each player personally every day…. You can be intense and competitive and all that, but try to remember to laugh and have fun. It's just a football game."

BY 1980, COACH MADDEN and Stabler were gone, but the Raiders continued to roll. That year, under new coach Tom Flores, Oakland started the decade in fine style by going 11–5 and pulling off three playoff upsets to reach the Super Bowl again. Few football experts gave the Raiders much of a chance against the powerful Philadelphia Eagles, but Oakland beat the odds and the Eagles 27–10 to give owner Al Davis a second world championship.

The two players most responsible for the Raiders' success that season were quarterback Jim Plunkett and cornerback Lester Hayes. Plunkett was a veteran whose career had seemed all but over when he joined the Raiders as a backup in 1978. Finally given an opportunity to play in the middle of the 1980 season, he seized it and never

A great rusher and receiver, Marcus Allen was one of the NFL's most versatile running backs.

looked back, becoming one of the most success-
ful quarterbacks in team history. Hayes, mean-
while, emerged as a star by making an incredible
13 interceptions during the season and five more
in the playoffs.

In 1982, to the disappointment of loyal Oakland
fans, the Raiders relocated south to Los Angeles.
Although the team had a strong following in
Oakland, Davis thought the Raiders would draw
more fans and make more money in the bigger Los
Angeles area. Another major story that year was the
addition of rookie Marcus Allen, a fast and shifty
running back from the University of Southern
California picked up in the NFL Draft.

The Raiders wasted no time winning over fans in
southern California. In 1983, they went 12–4 and
once again returned to the Super Bowl, a game
Allen turned into his personal showcase. The young
halfback carried the ball for 191 yards—including a sensational 74-yard touchdown run—as
L.A. trounced the Washington Redskins 38–9.
Although Allen would remain a Raiders star for
many seasons, few performances would match his
Super Bowl effort. "This has to be the greatest feel-
ing of my life," he said after the game. "I've been
to the Rose Bowl. I've won the Heisman Trophy
[as college football's best player]. But nothing is
sweeter than this."

EVEN THOUGH THE Raiders featured a number of exceptional players in the late 1980s—including Allen, tight end Todd Christensen, defensive end Howie Long, and cornerback Mike Haynes—the team slowly fell from the playoff picture. But in 1987, the excitement level rose a notch with the arrival of a new star: running back Vincent "Bo" Jackson.

Jackson spent only four seasons wearing Raiders silver and black, but he may well have been the most electrifying player in NFL history. At 6-foot-1 and 225 pounds, he had the speed of an Olympic sprinter and the strength of a lion. In a memorable Monday night game during his rookie year, Jackson ran for 221 yards against the Seattle Seahawks, leaving some defenders in his dust and simply flattening others.

Unbelievable speed and power made halfback Bo Jackson a football legend in just a few seasons.

Before a hip injury ended his football career in 1990, Jackson became the only NFL player ever to have two runs of more than 90 yards (91 and 92). As if that wasn't enough, he was also an All-Star outfielder for the Kansas City Royals professional baseball team. "I don't think there was a greater talent that put on a uniform," Kevin Seitzer, one of Jackson's Royals teammates, later said. "God knows how good he could have been if he would have concentrated on one sport."

After the excitement over Jackson died down, guard Steve Wisniewski and cornerback Terry McDaniel—under the leadership of new coach Art Shell, a former star offensive tackle for the Raiders—led L.A. to some solid seasons in the early 1990s. Then, the team returned to its roots when Davis decided to move the franchise back to Oakland in 1995. The city's passionate, black-clad fans enthusiastically welcomed their team home and made Network Associates Coliseum a raucous place even during the poor seasons that followed.

IN 1998, THE Raiders hired Jon Gruden as their new head coach. Gruden was just 34 years old—younger than a number of his players—but his fiery personality made him a fan favorite and seemed to bring out the best in his players. Over the course of the next few seasons, veteran quarterback Rich Gannon led an increasingly powerful offense, while young cornerback Charles Woodson emerged as a defensive standout.

Another Raiders star during those years was Tim Brown. The wide receiver and kick returner had joined the Raiders as a rookie in 1988, and even more than a decade later he seemed to have lost none of his speed or effectiveness. From 1993 to 2001, Brown posted more than 1,000 receiving yards every season and never ceased to amaze

Veteran Rich Gannon guided Oakland to the 2000 AFC title game and 2002 Super Bowl.

teammates with his great instincts and intelligence. "We call him 'The Natural,'" Gruden said. "You tell him one time, you show him one time, and you can expect perfection."

The first few seasons of the 21st century were memorable ones in Oakland. In 2000, the Raiders went 12–4 and reached the AFC championship game. The next year, they went 10–6 before losing to the New England Patriots in a playoff game famous for its controversy. Playing in a snowstorm in New England, the Raiders appeared to seal the victory when Woodson sacked Patriots quarterback Tom Brady late in the fourth quarter, forcing an apparent fumble that the Raiders recovered. After reviewing the play, however, officials ruled it an incomplete pass, and the Patriots eventually won 16–13 in overtime.

Although Gruden left town after the loss, the 2002 Raiders came back stronger than ever. Gannon had the finest season of his career, passing for an incredible 4,689 yards and 26 touchdowns to win the NFL Most Valuable Player award. The "over-the-hill" Raiders (Gannon and future Hall-of-Famers Brown, receiver Jerry Rice, and cornerback Rod Woodson were all in their late 30s) then won two playoff games to reach the Super Bowl for the first time in 19 years. Unfortunately, the Raiders fell short of the

Sebastian Janikowski was an Oakland fan favorite ^

championship, losing to the Tampa Bay Buccaneers and former coach Jon Gruden 48–21.

Despite the painful defeat and the disappointing 4–12 season that followed, Oakland fans were confident that a championship was still within reach. Although many of the team's stars were nearing retirement, such players as Charles Woodson, defensive tackle Warren Sapp, receiver Jerry Porter, and strong-legged kicker Sebastian Janikowski promised to keep the team among the AFC's elite.

The history of the Oakland Raiders is one of the NFL's great stories. Not only have the Raiders won almost 63 percent of their games since 1963 (the best winning percentage in pro football during that stretch), but they have won three Super Bowls and been represented by legendary players with such names as Otto, Snake, Assassin, and Bo. Today's Raiders stand ready to continue this tradition and make silver and black the color of champions once again.

Rod Woodson played his 17th NFL season in 2003 ^

INDEX>